1 o More

Pushups

- Complete Edition -

By Barry Rabkin

**Certified Sports Nutritionist & National
Council on Strength & Fitness Personal
Trainer**

Foreword by Nick Nilsson, Author of Muscle

Explosion and Mad Scientist Muscle

Please consult your doctor before starting any
exercise or nutrition program. We are not liable for
any injuries or damages. You train at your own risk.

Dedication

This book is proudly dedicated to all the brave men and women serving their countries in the military and law enforcement. Your strength inspires us all.

Table of Contents

Foreword by Nick Nilsson – Author of

Muscle Explosion and Mad Scientist Muscle

Foreword

The Push-Up is one of the classic tests of strength and muscular endurance. Practically every organization that tests the fitness of it's members or applicants uses the push-up as a measuring stick. And for good reason! It's true indicator of physical fitness.

And that's where Barry Rabkin and his book "How to Do More Push-Ups" comes in!

Barry has done a tremendous job explaining, dissecting and compiling all the information you need to take your push-up strength and endurance to a whole new level.

With the techniques and workouts found in this book, you will absolutely see amazing gains in your push-up numbers.

I've been in the fitness business more than 20 years and I still learned a lot from this book, especially about how to best take a push-up test. There are tips, tricks and techniques that not help you get ready for testing, but actually perform better during the test as well...and that can mean the difference between success or failure...acceptance or rejection.

If you're looking for a complete manual on how to do more push-ups, the title of this book really does say it all!

Nick Nilsson

Author of *Muscle Explosion - 28 Days to Maximum Mass, The Best Exercises You've Never Heard Of, and Mad Scientist Muscle*.

Nick has been weight training for more than 20 years and has been a certified personal trainer for 13 years. He holds a degree in Physical Education and Psychology.

#1 Introduction

"Knowledge is power." - Francis Bacon

"One can have no smaller or greater mastery than mastery of oneself." - Leonardo da Vinci

"Most powerful is he who has himself in his own power." - Seneca

"He who controls others may be powerful, but he who has mastered himself is mightier still." - Lao-Tzu

"I am, indeed, a king, because I know how to rule myself." - Pietro Aretino

Everyone would like to be able to do more pushups.
For some of us, it's an opportunity to increase our
fitness and physical mastery to finally reach a lifetime
goal, such as 50 pushups or even a one-handed
pushup. For some, it's a cheap, convenient, and
portable workout that we can do anytime and
anywhere. Many enjoy challenging friends, co-
workers, and family members to pushup contests,
either as a motivating challenge or as a
demonstration of strength and endurance.

For our men and women in the military and law
enforcement, pushups are a job requirement. The
following are the current men's **minimum** pushup
requirements for both the military and law
enforcement organizations. These numbers

represent what you must be able to complete before they will even consider admitting you. More are expected, and you should aim to do double these pushup numbers if you want to set yourself apart:

Delta Force - 55

FBI Hostage Rescue Team - 50

Army Ranger - 49

Air Force - 45

Navy - 42

National Guard - 35

ROTC - 35

Army Physical Fitness Test (APFT) - 35

FBI Special Agent - 30

Coast Guard – 29

To stand out, the maximum pushups for a perfect score on the men's Army Physical Fitness Test is 77 pushups in 2 minutes. No matter how qualified or dedicated you are, unless you meet the minimum requirements above, you will not be given an opportunity to serve. Fortunately, anyone can meet and exceed these goals, as long as you have the preparation, workout, and techniques that I will share with you.

I am certified as a National Council on Strength and Fitness personal trainer, and I have had the privilege of helping candidates apply to both the military and the Federal Bureau of Investigation, easily breezing through their physical fitness tests.

This book is broken into 5 sections:

1) Strategy and Goals - Choose your personal goals and customize your training to eliminate sticking points and maximize results!

2) Pushup Workouts - An exhaustively-tested collection of the most effective pushup workouts! Find your favorite or throw new challenges at your body for fresh gains every time!

3) Plateau Busters - Our bodies quickly adapt to our workouts and thrive off new challenges. These methods will let you blast through any plateau!

4) Pre-Test Preparation - Before your pushup test

or contest begins, prepare your mind and body to give their best performance!

5) Test Taking Technique - Do more pushups by improving the efficiency of your pushup form. Increase your stability and minimize wasted energy. Dramatically improve your performance by applying these techniques!

Whether doing more pushups for a job requirement, a workout, a personal goal, as part of a healthy lifestyle, or just for bragging rights, I will help you quickly break through your current limits to a new level of physical mastery, confidence, and power.

#2 Strategy and

Goals

"I have found that the more I prepare, the luckier I get." - Gary Player

Choose your personal goals and customize your training to eliminate sticking points and maximize your fast results!

Balance

Your body craves balance. If you have a strong chest and a weak back, not only will the imbalance look strange, it can causes injuries. If you only train pushups and neglect the rest of your body, it will be a sticking point. Your body wants to be proportional.

The 3 biggest muscles groups in your body are your chest, back, and legs. Even if pushups are your primary goal, make sure you exercise your back and leg muscle groups as well. Not only will you look more symmetrical, but it will keep your body growing consistently, burn more calories, stimulate more natural testosterone and growth hormone, and help prevent injuries.

Function Follows Form

Bad form will limit your progress and lead to injury.

If you can't do a pushup with good form yet, or if

you want to work up to doing advanced pushups like

clapping or one handed pushups, you can reduce the

difficulty of the pushup while maintaining perfect

form.

It can be hard to tell how good or bad your form is.

As you get tired, it's easy to let your hips or back sag

without realizing it. It's important to get feedback.

Use a mirror, video recordings, or a training partner

to check your form and identify problem areas. As

you become more aware of your body, you'll feel when something is out of alignment and be able to self correct.

Follow this progression for any difficult pushup you want to take on.

1) **Wall:** Start out by doing pushups while leaning against a wall and maintaining perfect form.

2) **Knees:** Then do pushups off your knees on the ground.

3) **Hands Up:** Then on an incline with your hands up on furniture. If you can do over 10 pushups that way, you'll be able to transition to doing some

standard pushup repetitions.

4) **Standard:** Then with standard pushup form flat on the ground.

5) **Feet Up:** If that gets to be too easy but you want to stick with that type of pushup, you can put your feet on a sturdy piece of furniture, placing more of your weight forward on your chest and shoulders.

6) **One Foot:** You can also lift your back foot in the air and do pushups off just one foot, putting more weight on your chest and challenging your core and back to stabilize you.

7) **Plyometric:** You can do plyometric pushups, such

as clapping pushups, in which you push off the ground hard enough to clap your hands in the air, between repetitions.

8) **One Hand:** Finally, you can do one-handed pushups, placing twice the demand on your muscles as normal.

These approaches can be combined with almost any pushup to make it easier or harder, and can even be combined with each other. Maybe you can't quite do a clapping pushup yet. That's okay, combine these strategies and practice doing clapping pushups off your knees.

Maybe a decline pushup is too easy for you. Maybe a

one-legged pushup is too easy for you. Maybe even a one-armed pushup is easy for you. Still, I've never met anyone who wasn't challenged, when attempting to do decline, one-legged, one-handed, explosive pushups!

For any pushup, you can make it easier or harder with these tricks to match your current level of ability; mix up your workouts; and keep them fresh, challenging, and fun.

Eliminate Your

Weakest Link

Maybe you can do 100 pushups, or maybe you can't even do one. No matter how strong or how weak we are, we all have stronger and weaker points. A pushup is a compound movement that requires several different, independent muscles to work together.

Like any chain, you are only as strong as your weakest link. If you give special focus in your workouts to the area that is giving out first, you can quickly improve that area so that it no longer limits your performance.

If you tend to struggle the most at the bottom of the pushups when your chest touches the ground, that means your chest muscles, your pectorals, are holding you back. If you tend to have the most

trouble in the top half off the movement, locking

out your arms to full extension, that means your arm

muscles, your triceps, are limiting you.

By focusing on those specific areas, you will make

faster progress. Wide pushups or low range of

motion pushups work your chest / pectorals,

whereas narrow diamond pushups or high range of

motion pushups emphasize your triceps.

If you want to build up strength in other areas, you

can focus on them by doing handstand pushups or

pike pushups to work your shoulders/deltoids,

decline pushups to work your upper chest/pectorals,

fist pushups to strengthen your forearms, or

fingertip pushups to strengthen your fingers.

Doing pushups to emphasize your weakest areas is a great way to eliminate your sticking points so that nothing is holding you back.

Grease the Groove

My friend Robert has the best strength to weight ratio of anyone I know. Surprisingly, he doesn't hit the gym or do planned workout routines.

Robert has a pullup bar installed in the doorway of his bedroom. Every time he goes in or out of his room, Robert does a quick set of pullups. He never pushes himself to muscular failure, but these short sets sprinkled throughout the day still add up. I've seen him effortlessly crank out over 30 pullups in a row without breaking a sweat! Robert's impressive endurance is all thanks to the quick sets that he does casually throughout his day.

Russian strength trainer Pavel Tsatsouline calls this technique "Greasing the Groove" or "GTG." In general, the more often we do something, the better we get at it. If you want to improve at piano or painting, you don't have to practice for a straight hour every day. Instead, you can practice for 20 minutes three times a day.

Exercises are also a skill that both our minds and

bodies adapt to with focused practice. You don't have to do endless marathon workouts to improve your strength or endurance. You can improve with light sets scattered throughout your day.

Aim for sets of 25%-50% of your maximum repetitions (your maximum is the highest number of pushups you can do continuously without stopping). So, if you max out at 40 pushups, when you "Grease the Groove" you'd do sets of 10-20 pushups, 3-4 times per day, 4-6 days per week.

As long as you don't train to to failure, you can keep training this way for multiple days in a row. That said, if you decide to train for 7-10 days straight, stop at that point and give your upper body 3-5 days off to fully recover from its accumulated wear and tear. After taking that time off, you'll come back even stronger!

Reps + Rest = Results

Most people assume that, if you get more muscle, you get stronger and that, if you get stronger, you get more muscle. That's true to a point, but it's not that simple. There are 200-pound power lifters that can bench press over 600 pounds, and there are body builders that weigh the same amount but can't lift half that.

What is your specific goal? Do you want to gain

strength so that you can be more competitive in your athletic weight class? Do you want size and to improve your physique rather than your athletic performance? Maybe you want a blend of both.

Once you pick your goal, you can train specifically for it by adjusting the difficulty of the move, the number of reps per set, and the rest between sets. Choose pushups challenging enough that you can work within these rep ranges with good form.

The more challenging the exercise you do, the more it will increase your strength; however, recognize that you will be completing fewer repetitions and will need more recovery. Use the following plans for what you want to focus on:

Strength - 5 set of 5 reps, with 2-5 minute rests

Size & Strength - 5 sets of 10 reps, with 60-120 second rests

Endurance - 5 sets of 15 reps, with 60-90 second rests

Fat Loss - 5 sets of 20 reps, with 30-60 second rests

Keep Records

Keep records for motivation - It's easy to forget how

many pushups you did last time or how many you could do when you started. Keep a log of your workouts. It will also push you to go a little further every workout.

If you're doing standard pushups, you can just write the date and the reps for each set. If you want to take it to the next level, write down your rests between sets, the type of workouts (if you're mixing it up) and notes on how the workout went.

Keep records to spot trends - Everyone is different, so different tricks will work for each of us. Keep notes to help you see what leads to your best and worst workouts. Maybe a particular pre-workout meal, song, time of day, gym, or training partner help you get your best results. Maybe every time that you stay up late you're tired and have a bad workout the next day.

Everyone is different, so find out what works best for you. Check your workout records for trends. Repeat what gives you good workouts and cut out what doesn't.

Keep records to avoid plateaus—nothing works forever. If you repeat the same workout too many times, your results will plateau. Likewise, if you don't give your body recovery time between workouts, you'll get weaker, not stronger. Keeping records is a great way to catch these issues.

If you see your results taper off, that's a warning sign that something needs to change. You might need a break to let your muscles recover. Or, you might need to mix it up with fresh exercises. Keeping records lets you to see when it's time for a change and act accordingly.

Wanna Bet?

Nothing motivates me more than a friendly wager. The minute you bet me 5 bucks on something, I will go to the ends of the earth to win. You can challenge a friend, classmate, family member, or co-worker to a bet that you can do more pushups than they can in a month. Put something at stake like a free home cooked dinner, some cash, or that night's drinks and pizza.

Even if your challenger is at a dramatically different level of fitness than you, the playing field can be leveled. Just bet that the stronger one has to do 2 pushups or a clapping pushup for every standard pushup the other one does. That way, it's balanced but still competitive.

Never Be Sore Again:

Workout Secrets

Soreness is a natural result of pushing your muscles

harder than they are used to. It comes from swelling and aching from micro-tears in the muscle contracting forcefully against your body weight.

If you are so sore that it's hard to move and you have to skip workouts, these tricks will help. Your soreness, and the amount of time you need to recover, directly increase with the intensity of the workout. If you want to be less sore and recover faster, you have a few options.

Do fewer reps, fewer sets, less weight, or longer rests. There is no universally **"hard"** workout for everyone, it's all relative to what your body is used to. Results come quickly for beginners, and if you're just starting out on an exercise plan, what's almost impossible today might be easy by next month.

If you normally do a set of 20 pushups 3 times a week, you'll be able to do 25 without feeling like Barry Bonds took a bat to your chest the next day. If you normally do 20 pushups and you do 200, expect you arms and chest to feel like jello for a few days.

Pushing past your normal workouts is essential for encouraging growth, but it's easiest to do with incremental progress, not giant jumps. You're better off adding a few more pushups each week, rather than going a month without exercise and trying to make up for it by doing a month worth of workouts in one session. You'll be so sore that you'll never want to work out again.

There are a bunch of easy changes you can make so that a workout won't leave you overly sore:

- You can decrease the number of repetitions per set. For example, if you normally do 10 reps, stop short at 8.

- You can do fewer total sets. If you would normally do 5 sets of 10 repetitions, this time just do 3 sets of 10 repetitions.

- Taking longer rests between sets gives your muscles more time to recuperate. If you normally take 1 minute between sets, try taking 2 minutes.

- Finally, switching to less intense exercises will make you less sore. If clapping one- handed pushups left you too sore to crawl out of bed, do the same workout next time but with standard pushups. If standard pushups crushed you, do the same workout but off your knees in order to decrease the intensity.

You will still gain strength from the workout, but this way you can amp up your strength with steady gains, rather than trying huge leaps that your body isn't ready for.

Never Be Sore Again:

Post-Workout Secrets

You can massively decrease your post-workout soreness without changing your workout by using the following tricks:

- Do cardio for 10-20 minutes after lifting. This will help oxygenate your worked muscles. After a workout, light cardio, such as jogging or doing jumping jacks for 20 minutes, can reduce soreness by as much as 50%.

- Stretch for 10-20 minutes after lifting. Your muscles contract and tighten when you challenge them. It took more than 5 seconds to get them sore, so it will take more than 5 seconds to stretch them. To get the best results, hold each stretch for at least 1-2 minutes in order to relax the muscle fully.

- For pushups, the most important stretches are your chest (pectorals), shoulders (deltoids) and arms (triceps).

- To stretch your chest, stand by a wall or doorway. Place the inside of your bent arm against the surface. Begin with your elbow at shoulder height. Lower your elbow to stretch your upper chest or raise your elbow to stretch your lower chest. The picture below shows how to stretch your right arm against a wall. Do this for both arms. Hold the stretch for 30-90 seconds and repeat until

your chest loosens up.

Chest Stretch - Hold your bent arm against a wall and turn away from it.

- To stretch your shoulder, stick your arm out

  and cross it horizontally across your chest,

  and pull your arm towards you with your free

  hand, holding it between your elbow and

tricep. The following pictures shows how to stretch your right shoulder. Do this for both arms. Hold the stretch for 30-90 seconds and repeat until they loosen up.

Shoulder Stretch #1 - Stick your arm straight out in front of you.

Shoulder Stretch #2 - Pull your arm across your chest with your free arm.

- To stretch your tricep, take your hand and touch your opposite shoulder blade. Now lean back against the arm with your head and stabilized the stretched arm at the elbow with your free hand. The pictures below shows how to stretch your right tricep. Do this for both arms. Hold the stretch for 30-90 seconds and repeat until they loosen up.

Hair of the Dog

that Bit You

According to Scottish folklore, if a rabid dog bites you, you can place a few hairs from that dog in the wound to prevent rabies and grant you a swift recovery. Likewise, if a workout makes you sore, getting a small amount of the same exercise will actually help you recover faster!

This is not folklore, light repetitions of the exercise that made you sore will flush the muscle with nutrient and oxygen rich blood.

If you did too many clapping one handed pushups

or hit the bench press too hard yesterday, and your chest feels like it was trampled by wild horses, do a few sets (10 repetitions per set) of pushups off your knees. You can do light versions of any difficult exercise to aid in your recovery.

Kill Your Cortisol

During a workout, you use up your energy stores, leaving your body in a depleted state. When under physical or mental stress, your body secretes a hormone called cortisol. Cortisol breaks down muscle and lowers your testosterone levels. To drop your cortisol levels after a workout, get a healthy, well-rounded meal or drink a shake within 20 to 60 minutes of your workout.

Rest for Your Test

You don't get bigger and stronger from your workout. Your diet, rest, and recovery are what help you come back stronger. It's important to get a full night's sleep of 8 or more hours after you workout. If you're only getting 5 or 6 hours of sleep, you won't be able to push yourself as hard in your workouts, and it will take much longer for your body to recover from your workouts, and grow stronger.

Drink at least 8-12 glasses of water or electrolyte (potassium and sodium) enriched sports drinks during and after your workouts so your system stays fresh, balanced, and well hydrated.

If you have a fitness test Friday, you don't want to start training Thursday night. Start weeks or months before your test and then take a few days off before the test. Try to leave at least 3-5 days between your last workout and the time of your pushup test.

After that point, anything you do will break down the muscle without leaving you time to fully recover, so you'll be going into the test weaker, not stronger. You're better off skipping last minute workouts and going in completely fresh.

Alcohol vs. Athlete

While alcohol will not help your muscle gaining goals, an occasional drink in moderation won't sabotage your results.   Plenty of world class athletes still enjoy having a beer or glass of wine now and then.

Just try to avoid binge drinking as the over consumption of alcohol has been shown to reduce testosterone, reduce growth hormone, increase cortisol, increase the storage of fat, and slow muscle growth and repair.

If you do drink alcohol, consume plenty of water and electrolytes before you go to sleep so you can help your body flush out the alcohol and restore the fluids that you lost from the diuretic, dehydrating effect of alcohol.

Practice Perfection

There is no single, universally agreed upon definition of perfect pushup form. If you're training to meet specific testing requirements, get the exact expectations that they demand and train exactly the way you'll be tested.

The *Guinness Book of World Records* requirement for pushups is to bend your arms and go down until your elbows are bent 90 degrees. Many military and law enforcement physical tests demand that you go down until your chest hits the instructor's fist on the ground beneath you. Some fitness tests require that you to bring your chest or your nose to the ground.

If you miss the ground or instructor's fist by a hair, that repetition isn't counted and that time and energy was wasted. Whatever the test requires, find out and train for it so that you get in the physical and mental habit of doing pushups that way.

You can also use props like a baseball, or a few books under your chest to simulate bringing your chest down to the test instructor's fist, so, when the test comes, you'll be mentally and physically prepared with no surprises.

Visualize

"You become what you think about." - Earl Nightingale

After years of hard training a 150 pound power lifter can squat 500 pounds, which is much more than most people twice their weight.

Even without gaining weight, you can lift more by having better mental control of your muscles. Every physical movement that you make is controlled by electrical signals from your brain.

When you intensely visualize yourself going through an exercise or movement, you activate the same parts of your brain as when you actually do the motion.

The stronger your mental signal for the movement is, the more easily your body will be able to do it.

Visualizing works best on moves that you know somewhat but want to improve on and do more easily with more energy. Before you do an exercise, close your eyes and picture yourself doing it perfectly. Think about how every body part moves and feels as you complete the movement.

"All that we are is the result of what we have thought. The mind is everything. What we think we become." - Buddha

You can do this to practice any move anytime, anywhere. When you visualize, you never get tired, you always do the move perfectly and you don't even break a sweat.

You can visualize while you're in study hall, waiting for a bus or getting ready to fall asleep. The more vividly you can visualize the movement, and the more often you visualize the movement between training sessions or during a practice before you actually do the move, the easier actually doing it will become for you!

Many of the best athletes, gymnasts, power lifters, and dancers that I know practice movements in their head throughout the day and before they go to sleep. When they go to actually do a move in practice, they have already visualized themselves doing it perfectly hundreds of times since their last training session.

These mental rehearsal shows increase their progress in learning new moves and allow them to feel complete confidence when they are performing.

"If I can't picture it, then I can't understand it." - Albert Einstein

If you don't understand a move mentally, then you can't do it physically. Watching videos of the movement in slow motion repeatedly will help you understand the movement. After that, you'll need to picture yourself doing the move in your head.

Focus on every aspect of the move and where each of your limbs are at each part of the move. Next, speed up and slow down the move in your head and focus on how each part feels. After you make a mistake in real life, visualize yourself doing the move perfectly to recalibrate.

With mental familiarity with the move, you'll be able to do it physically with a fraction of the time and effort. Unlike real life, your brain never gets tired or injured, and you can practice anytime, anywhere!

#3 Pushup

Workouts

"Before I get in the ring, I'd have already won or lost it out on the road. The real part is won or lost somewhere far away from witnesses- behind the lines, in the gym and out there on the road long before I dance under those lights." –

Muhammad Ali

Get ready for a in depth collection of the most effective pushup workouts! Find your favorite, or throw new challenges at your body for fresh gains every workout!

21s

21s are a great way to emphasize the muscles used at different phases of a movement. Start out by doing 7 repetitions of the bottom half of a pushup, followed by 7 repetitions of the 2nd repetitions of the top half of a pushup, and finish it off with 7 repetitions of the complete movement.

This first works your chest, then your triceps. Besides singling out those muscles, this also forces you to use excellent form, since you can't let momentum help you over such a limited range of motion. 21s can be extended to almost any exercise and are a simple and surprisingly challenging way to vary your routine.

Beat the Clock

First, time how long it takes you to do a set amount of reps, like 100 pushups. Next, time yourself rushing to reach the same number in less time. So, if last time you did 100 pushups in a half hour, this time try to do it in 28 minutes, and next time in 26 minutes.

For every workout that you cut your time, you're decreasing your rest time and increasing the muscular and conditioning intensity of the workout.

Make the Most

of Your Time

Set the clock for a given amount of time, say 30 minutes, and do as many reps as you can in that time. Try to do a few more reps in the same amount of time every workout. So, if last time you did 100 pushups in 30 minutes, this time aim for 105 pushups, and then 110 pushups next time. Keep upping your goal repetitions and your strength and endurance will increase steadily as your workouts progress.

More Reps - Record how many repetitions you did in that amount of time and try to set a new record next time. So, if you did 500 in an hour last workout, this time try for 510 pushups, and 520 pushups the time after that. Even if you just add a single pushup every workout, your endurance will improve very quickly.

Less Time - For every workout, try to hit the same number of repetitions but in less time. So, if you did 500 pushups in 60 minutes last workout, try to hit 500 pushups in just 57 minutes this time. That might not sound like much of a challenge, but it would only take 10 times adjusting your workouts like that to get you from doing 500 pushups in 60 minutes to doing 500 pushups in just 30 minutes, **doubling** your strength, speed, and endurance. Smaller time adjustments are fine, even cutting a minute each workout will get you fast results.

Less Sets - Try to hit the same total number of repetitions in fewer sets. Even doing the same exact number of repetitions can be much more challenging if you do it in fewer sets. After all, which is harder doing 1 uninterrupted set of 100 pushups in a row, or 5 sets of 20 pushups with long rests in between?

So, if last time, you did 500 pushups in 50 sets of 10 repetitions each, this time try to do 500 pushups in sets of 11 repetitions each. Adding a single rep might not sound like much, but, when it's multiplied across over 45 sets, it catches up to you!

Less Rest - Cut the rest between sets. If last time

you set a timer to ring every 120 seconds and did a

set, this time set a timer and try to do a set of

pushups every 110 seconds. It's amazing how much

more difficult the workout becomes as you reduce

your rest time! You can fine tune the speed and

increase the difficulty of these methods to suit your

needs, but these general examples should help you

get started!

Pyramids

Using the pyramid method, you will do a long series

of sets that will progressively increase and decrease

over time. You will gradually increase the quantity

of repetitions that you do on each set, until you can't

do any more. Then, after you've maxed out and can't

increase your repetitions further, you'll gradually reduce repetitions on each set.

For example, you'd do 5 pushups then rest a minute; do 10 pushups and rest a minute; max out at 15 pushups and rest a minute; do 10 pushups, rest a minute, and then finish off with 5 final pushups. This is a great way to build muscular endurance, get a serious pump, and push your body fully through a high volume workload of strength building repetitions.

Relays

If you've got over 15 feet of open space to work

with and a training partner, relays are a great way to improve your muscular endurance and stimulate your testosterone. Motivation from a partner will help you stay motivated and giving it everything you've got. Don't worry about counting the number of repetitions of the movement you do, just focus on traveling from one side of the room to the other as quickly and explosively as you can. Take any traveling pushup, such as clapping pushups, and starting at one wall travel forward across the floor, doing the movement until you reach the opposite wall. Immediately turn around and head back, continuing to travel while doing pushups.

As soon as you return to your partner, slap their hand and rest while they head out and come back again to slap your hand ,and than you start off again.

Relays self adjust, they automatically give you more

rest the longer distance you travel, since it will take

longer for your partner to travel out and back.

If you would like more rest, just add more partners,

so that, instead of resting for one relay and moving

for one relay, you rest while you wait for 2 or 3

partners to complete their relay before it's your turn

to do the relay again.

If you want to have a contest, get a few teams

together, set a timer, and see which team can

complete the most relays before the timer goes off.

This workout works for any traveling movement,

including jump squats, crap walks, burpies or lunges.

Rep Targeting

This is a great workout to do while watching a movie or television show. Pick a large total number of times to perform any strength training exercise and your workout isn't over until you hit that number! Some of the most popular exercises for rep targeting are pushups, squats, jump squats, clapping pushups, and sit ups.

You want to choose a number that is challenging, but realistic for you to complete in 20-60 minutes. For example, if you can do 25 pushups in a row, you could make 200 pushups your rep target for your workout.

If you mainly want to focus on cardiovascular health and fat loss, you can consistently bang out a few reps with short 30-60 seconds rests in between to keep your heart rate up. If you mainly want to focus on improving your strength take longer 2-5 minute rests in between sets and do a higher numbers of repetitions.

As you make progress, you can go for a higher number of reps, or try to reach the same number in a new record time. This is a great technique to build endurance, stimulate testosterone, break through plateaus on stubborn body parts, and give you a huge pump.

However, be aware that, if you target an unusually high volume of reps, you are likely to be extremely sore for 1-3 days after. You can minimize this by sipping a carb and protein shake during and after your workout. Finishing your workout with 10-20 minutes of light cardio and stretching will help bring more nutrient rich blood to your muscles to help them growth and repair.

Rest Reduction

Anyone can do any amount of pushups if they have enough time. As long as you can do a single pushup, you can do 100 pushups, if you take enough breaks and give yourself enough time. This is the key to rest reduction, you're going to find a number of reps with a pace that you can sustain and slowly decrease your rest time to increase the challenge.

For example, you'd start out by setting a timer and doing 10 pushups, then resting 120 seconds between sets. Next workout, do the same 10 pushups per set, but only rest 110 seconds between sets. Next workout, go down to 100 seconds. Even though you're doing the same number of pushups, every time that you cut the rest period down, you're increasing your challenge and your endurance.

Tabata Drills

Tabata drills use incredibly intense, fast interval training to build cardiovascular endurance, burn fat, and give you a great workout in a minimum amount of time. You can use any continuous movement for Tabata, including pushups, squats, running, biking, or jumping rope. You follow a specific structure of 20 seconds of exercise, followed by a 10 second rest, and repeat this for a total of 8 cycles in 4 minutes.

Your Tabata score for that exercise is the lowest number of repetitions you could do for any set. So, if you do a Tabata drill for pushups ,you'll do as many pushups as you can in 20 seconds, rest for 10 seconds, and repeat that sequence 8 times. Your score is the lowest number of pushups you did in any of the 8 sets, and you can try to beat your score every time. Nowadays, Tabata Timers and smart phone apps are easy to find. While they may sound simple, Tabata Drills are proven to be one of the most effective ways to quickly drop fat, improve conditioning, and build muscular endurance.

Tag Team

Tag Teaming is one of the most intense training techniques known to humankind because it tells your muscles to either get bigger or fall off the bone. It's not for the faint of heart, or for inexperienced athletes.

You pick one exercise and perform it non-stop with

one partner, so whenever one of you stops, the next

one starts. This style of training is generally done

with 10-20 sets, and, even if you are doing an

exercise that you can usually perform easily, by your

10th set you will be gasping for breath.

If you and your partner have similar levels of

endurance, that will work well; however, if you are at

very different training levels, that will even out too.

For instance, the less reps that you can do, the

shorter their rest will be, and the more reps that your

partner can do, the longer your reps will be, so,

within a few sets as your rests are longer and theirs

are shorter, you will naturally equalize.

As you and your partner get tired and your sets get

shorter and shorter, that makes your rests shorter and shorter as well, so this format is great for building endurance, burning fat, and improving your cardiovascular health.

For example, the first person would do 25 pushups while the other rests. Now his/her partner goes and does 25 while the first one rests. For the next set, trainee #1 can only do 18, and, as soon as he stops, #2 starts and does 17, as soon as #2 stops #1 is back up and does 15, and so on.

One of you is always resting while the other trains, and you keep alternating back and forth, so training is being continuously performed throughout your session. You can also make it easier by doing this rotating around 3 or 4 partners, so, as soon as 1 stops, 2 starts and, as soon as 2 stops, 3 starts and so on.

More partners allows for more rest time for each person and is recommended for beginners and for extremely challenging exercises, which will require more recovery time between sets.

Volume Training

With volume training, your goal is to do the most possible repetitions of the movement in the workout by doing a huge number of sets with a small number of repetitions per set. Doing 30% of your normal maximum repetitions is a good place to start.

So, if you can do 100 straight pushups, for volume training just do sets of 30 pushups but do 10 sets of them. Therefore, by the end of your workout, instead of your normal 100 pushups, you'll have done 300 total pushups—triple the workload your body is used to!

The lower rep sets allow you to stay mentally and physically fresher and do many more total repetitions than just doing 1 or 2 sets until muscular failure. It also trains you for success instead of failure because, since you aren't forcing yourself to go until you drop, your body gets used to completing every rep it attempts. Volume training with low reps and high sets is a great way to stimulate growth, increase your

muscular endurance, and train your body to do more

reps with good form because placing a larger

workload on your muscles encourages growth.

#4 Plateau

Busters

"What does not kill me, makes me stronger." -

Friedrich Nietzsche

Our bodies quickly adapt to our workouts and thrive off new challenges. These methods will let you blast through any plateau!

2-Up 1-Down Negatives

Slowly lowering your body weight or a weight is a great way to build strength and lose weight—this is called negative training or negatives. It allows you to push the muscle far past the point of positive failure when you could not complete another normal repetition.

The problem is that, unless you have a spotter, as you tire your muscle with this exercise, you won't be able to pick up the weight, or your body weight again to lower it. The way around this is 2-Up/1 Down negatives.

Use both limbs to push and just one limb to slowly

lower yourself down. For example, get into a one-handed pushup position with your arm fully extended and lower yourself down as slowly as you possibly can, once you reach the bottom of the movement, push yourself back up with both hands.

Now you're back where you started and you can go back through the cycle, lowering yourself down again. Do this as many times as you can until you stop being able to lower yourself with control, then switch arms.

You can do squats the same way, lower yourself on one leg, stand back up using both legs and repeat. You also do a modified version of negatives for pullups, chin ups, and dips. You'd use your legs to jump up to the top of the movement, then slowly lower yourself down with your upper body, jump up to the top of the movement with your legs, and repeat.

If you want to put yourself through the most punishing workout of your life, do a combined Negative Drop Set: After you can no longer lower yourself with control, immediately switch to an easier exercise and squeeze out more reps.

For example, get into a one-handed pushup position with your arm fully extended and lower yourself down as slowly as you possibly can. Once you reach the bottom of the movement, push yourself back up with both hands, and lower yourself again with the one arm. Do this as many times as you can, until you stop being able to lower yourself with control, then switch to doing them with your hands on a piece of furniture to take more weight off your arms.

Then, when you can't do that anymore, switch to doing them flat on the ground off your knees. A few drop set negative sequences are a true test of will. They are enough to leave anyone sore for days, but they are also one of the best challenges you can give your body to encourage fresh growth.

Aftershock

After you're done with your primary workout, you can do a final easy sequence to fill your muscles with nutrient rich blood. For example, after 3 sets of 20 clapping pushups, you could do 3 sets of 10 pushups off your knees.

The light exercise will pump blood into the muscle and prime it for recovery and growth. Be sure to stop short of failure, the goal with this technique is to deliver nutrients to your muscles to help them recover, not to further tear the muscle down.

Failure Is Only

the Beginning

After you hit muscular failure, a spotter can help take some of the weight off your muscle to help you force out a few more repetitions. For example, if you're doing chinups and you can't do anymore, a spotter could help lift up your feet to allow you to complete a few more reps.

Alternately you can do assisted reps, place a chair beneath your chinup bar, and push off with your feet to help you finish more reps.

Another popular method is self spotting with single

limb exercises. For example, if your doing one-armed pushups, and you can't do anymore, you can take your free hand and push off the ground very slightly, just enough so that you can take some of the weight off and finish a few more repetitions of one-armed pushups.

You can gently take some weight off the hand doing most of the work to push it well past normal muscular failure. This works great for one-legged squats, one-arm pushups, one-arm chin ups, one-arm dumbbell bicep curls, one-arm dumbbell shoulder press, one-arm dumbbell bench press, one-arm dumbbell row, and virtually any single limb exercise, and you don't need a spotter to safely push yourself past the point of muscular failure into fresh gains.

Hands Off

In many pushup tests, you have to bring your chest all the way to the ground or it doesn't count. As you get tired, it's tempting to cheat. People often fail to go through the complete range of motion and don't even realize it. I've found a great technique to keep yourself honest.

Between every pushup, pick your hands up completely off the ground. That means you literally have to touch your chest to the ground, put all your weight on your chest, take your hands completely off the ground, and press back into a new pushup.

This **completely** eliminates the risk of cheating, shallow repetitions, and relying on momentum because it forces you to do every pushup with a full range of motion.

In US military pushup tests your hands are never allowed to come up off the ground, so this method should be reserved strictly as an intense training technique, not an in-test habit. But you wouldn't want to do this during a test anyhow since it makes your range of motion and workload so much harder than normal pushups.

Muscular Overload

We all know workouts make us stronger, but most of us don't know exactly how or why. When we contract our muscles against resistance, the strain puts micro-tears in the muscle tissue. The more the muscle is challenged, the more micro-tears it gets.

The muscle responds to the punishment by healing, and coming back stronger to protect itself from future abuse. After you recover, the micro-tears will be patched with freshly added muscle so that you can lift a little more a little longer.

One way to create these micro-tears is to simply do more pushups so that your muscles spend more time under tension. Another way is to increase the amount of resistance the muscle fibers have to push against so that they get more micro-tears during the same number of pushups.

By having a training partner put a weight plate on your back, push on your back, sit on your back, or by using a resistance band, a weight vest, or a sturdy backpack loaded with books or weights, you can dramatically increase the resistance that your muscles have to push against.

Get your body used to doing pushups with more than your actual body weight. Then, when you switch to doing pushups with just your body and no added resistance, you will feel light and you'll be able to do many more repetitions than before.

Odds & Evens

Stew Smith is a former Navy SEAL and certified strength and conditioning specialist. Myself and many others have seen rapid increases to our pushup numbers by following Smith's 10-day boot camp pushup plan.

Unlike most plans that give you breaks to recover between workouts, with this one you're going to be doing pushups every single day for 10 straight days. This works on the same principle as the "Grease the Groove" method in Chapter 2. Your target number of pushups each day will depend on your current level of endurance. If you can do under 75 pushups without stopping, your target is 200 pushups a day. If you can do over 75 pushups in a row, your target is 300 pushups a day.

On odd days (1,3,5,7,9) do your target number of pushups in as few sets as possible. If you can do 40 pushups, try to hit 200 pushups in a **low number** of **maximum repetition sets.** For example, you could do 200 pushups in 4 sets of 50 repetitions.

On even days (2,4,6,8,10) you'll do the opposite. Do your target number of pushups in a **high number** of **low repetition sets** evenly spread out throughout the day. If you can do 40 pushups, you could hit your 200 pushup total with 20 sets of 10 pushups throughout the day. If you can do 80 pushups, you could hit your 300 pushup total with 20 sets of 15 throughout the day. You can increase or decrease the size of your sets, just stay under 50% of your maximum pushups (the most pushups you can do continuously without stopping.)

This accelerated workout plan will break your body down faster than it can recover, so at the end of the 10 days you'll need to give your upper body 3-5 days of complete rest in order to fully heal. After recovery, many people can perform 10%-50% more maximum pushups than when they started. Because of this plan's intensity, it's only recommended once every 6 months. But, if you want fast results, this is a powerful way to make the maximum progress in the minimum time!

Partials / Burns

After you can't do anymore of pushups with good form, squeeze out some pushups just working through a few inches of the movement. For example, after you can't do anymore complete pushups with good form, you'd lower yourself half-way down and squeeze out a few more partial repetitions with a limited range of motion to squeeze everything out of the muscle.

Plyometrics

Plyometrics are great for improving your explosive power. If you want to train for a single explosive movement like a high jump or long jump, you should train differently than someone who needs to run a long steady series of challenges like a marathon or hurdles. You can use plyometrics to make your upper body more explosive too.

If plyometrics in a standard pushup position are too hard, you can start out by doing them leaning forward against a wall or flat on the ground off your knees. You start by pushing yourself off the ground hard enough to clap your hands together between repetitions. When that gets too easy, you can clap further and further away from the ground to increase the challenge. Try clapping behind your back, over your head, and slapping your knees if you need more of a challenge as your explosiveness increases. Use plyometrics challenging enough that you can work within these rep ranges:

Explosive Endurance - 4 sets of 12 rep sets with 60-90 second rests.

Explosive Strength - 4 sets of 8 Reps with 60-120 second rests.

Explosive Power - 5 set of 1-5 reps, with 2-5 minute rests.

Pre-Exhaust

Do More Pushups

This is particularly good for blasting a specific problem area. Let's say your arms tend to give out, and you've been having trouble locking out your pushups at the top of the movement. You want to really focus on forcing your arms to grow, so start by doing a set of diamond pushups to pre-exhaust your triceps, then follow it up with a set of standard pushups.

Your fresh chest will allow you further work your already tired triceps and push them past the point that they could not do anymore standard pushups. Likewise, you could do a set of bicep curls, then do chinups to further challenge them. This technique works for any compound exercise that involves multiple muscle groups working together.

Rest-Pause

The goal of rest-pause is to give yourself just enough recovery time to squeeze out another few extra reps. For instance, if your doing clapping pushups and you can't do anymore with good form, wait 5-10 seconds, catch your breath, and then squeeze out a few more. Finally, take another short rest and repeat more reps.

This gets hard fast, but you can always squeeze out another rep or two after a short break. Not allowing yourself a complete rest will help stimulate testosterone and forces your muscles to increase their energy reserves and endurance.

Do the Twist

If you throw a punch forward, you'll notice that your wrist and knuckles naturally twist in toward your body as you fully extend your arm. When you twist your wrist, you should also twist your shoulders in towards your chest and reverse shrug your shoulders down towards your chest to help stabilize your body.

To do a reverse shrug, shrug your shoulders up, like you're trying to touch your ears with your shoulders. Now do the opposite and push your shoulders down as far as you can. This lets your shoulders lock your upper body in to place so your chest and triceps don't have to work as hard to keep your body steady.

#1 Rotate your shoulders in towards your chest.

#2 Reverse shrug your shoulders down to stabilize your body.

#1 Rotate your shoulders in towards your chest.

#2 Reverse shrug your shoulders down to stabilize your body.

Pushups don't normally let you maintain this natural turning movement because your hands are firmly locked into place on the ground and can't turn.

Locking their hands in place causes many people to experience wrist, elbow and shoulder pain when they do pushups and severely restricts their training volume.

Fortunately, there is an easy way around this problem. Get yourself a pair of Perfect Pushups™. They are low-friction turning platforms that allow your arms to turn through their natural range of motion as you do your pushups.

Rotating your hands is easier if you have access to a

low-friction tile, stone, wood, vinyl, or linoleum floor. Or if you're on a budget you can do rotating pushups with your hands in socks or placed on hand towels.

When you train with twisting pushups, you'll be able to rotate your hands in and out and follow your bodies natural movements. If joint pain has been holding you back, now you can finally push your limits, make fast progress, and shatter your old pushup record!

Even if you have to take your test or contest without wrist rotation, the strength and endurance you build up with twisting pushups will transfer over to standard pushups.

In fact, even if you don't experience any joint pain from pushups, the rotating movement gives your stabilizing muscles an extra challenge holding your body steady as you turn. When you train with a twist and then switch back to normal pushups, you will feel light and your developed stabilizing muscles will keep your body tight and strong.

#5 Pre-Test

Preparation

"Well begun is half done." - Aristotle

Before your pushup test or contest begins, prepare

your mind and body to give their best possible

performance!

Break a Sweat

Your heart and body can't go from resting to a

maximum output instantly. It takes your heart, veins

and muscles time to fully dilate and gradually prepare

themselves for battle. By doing light cardio and

getting your blood pumping, you slowly prepare your

body to give its all and release adrenaline, speeding

up your heart rate to provide you with more energy.

Don't walk into a pushup test cold, it will catch your

body off guard and you'll run out of energy quickly.

Warm up with jumping jacks, jump roping, or

jogging on the side for 5-15 minutes. Once you

break a good sweat and your body and mind are

ready, you'll be fully prepared for your best possible

performance on your test.

Fight or Flight?

Adrenaline is a powerful stimulant similar to caffeine
and it can make you feel edgy and nervous. When
your mind tells your body that it's got a demanding
physical task coming up, your body releases
adrenaline, which increases your blood flow and
switches your pounding heart to turbo mode. Your
body crosses over to its primitive caveman survival
instincts and assumes that it is getting ready for a
fight or to run away from a predator.

You know you're really just getting ready for your
pushup test, but it's easy to interpret your

lightheadedness and thumping heartbeat as nervousness or fear. When you think that you are stressed or nervous, you will feel even more nervous, which is a vicious cycle that gets worse and worse.

You can break the cycle simply by being aware that what you're feeling is natural and that everyone experiences it. This is not caused by nervousness, it's just your body getting ready to perform. Remind yourself that what you're feeling is simply pent-up excitement and energy that you're going to release during your pushup test.

Your heart's beating hard, your adrenaline is rushing through your veins, and your body is getting ready to give its all. Your body's preparing itself for a physical encounter, which is exactly what you want.

Remind yourself that these feelings are just your body getting ready for your best possible performance. This excitement and energy is a good sign that you'll have tons of energy, not a bad sign of nervousness or stress. Focusing on taking slow, deep breaths will help you slow your heart rate down and calm your nerves.

With a sudden spike of adrenaline from stress or exercise, your heart can jump from 60 beats per minute to 200 in less than a half second. At just 145 heart beats per minute, most people begin to lose their complex motor skills, such as hand-eye coordination and timing, making efficient pushups difficult or completely impossible.

Breathing control techniques can help you recover from the effects of adrenaline and slow your heart rate down. Breathe in through your nose, hold the air in, and then breath out through your mouth. Break your breathing into three parts—inhaling, holding, and exhaling—with a four count pause for each step.

To slow your heart rate down, realize that your excitement and racing heart rate are completely natural and do the following for two to ten minutes to get your body back in a calmer, more focused state:

Inhale for a four count.

Hold your breath for a four count.

Exhale for a four count.

These tips will help you slow your heart rate down and focus your mind on success.

Meditate

If you have a pushup test or a pushup contest, take some time beforehand to focus. Take a few quiet minutes to quietly meditate by yourself and visualize yourself giving your best performance.

You can't win every contest, but you can always give

100% of what you have to give at that moment.

Tune out everything around you, and just focus on giving it everything you've got.

If you are just out to win, you might get intimidated if someone else performs well. Don't worry about winning, you can't control that. Just focus on giving it everything you have.

That's all anybody could ever ask of you, and that's in your power to give. Not only will you always have your pride, your focus and mindset will often bring you victory!

Work to Rest

Opposing muscle groups control opposite motions. For example, in a pushup, your chest muscles push your arms forward in front of you, while in a rowing motion your back muscles pull your arms back toward you.

When you work a muscle in one direction, your body automatically forces the opposite muscle group to release tension, relax, and recharge so that the muscles don't fight each other. You can use this knowledge and work opposing muscle groups to recover faster for pushups.

You just want to push yourself to the limit or you may deplete your endurance and energy stores. By working your back, your goal is purely to help your chest and triceps fully relax during the break so that you can squeeze out even more reps afterward.

For example, when you're training pushups, between sets, or before you start doing pushups for your test or contest, you can do some pullups, Australian pullups, or dumbbell rows, which work your back muscles and force your chest muscles to relax.

When you come back to do more pushups, your chest and tricep muscles will actually be fresher and more relaxed than if you'd just rested, and the extra exercise will improve your cardiovascular fitness and burn extra calories.

Post-Activation

Potentiation

Your body doesn't normally enlist all of its muscle fibers at once. If it did, when you went to lift up a fork, you'd automatically engage every muscle and throw the fork over your head. Your body only enlists as many muscle fibers as it thinks it needs, but you can trick it into activating more muscle fibers than necessary to make an exercise feel light.

If you lift a piece of paper and then lift a 1 pound weight, the 1 pound weight will feel heavy. If you lift a 10 pound weight and then lift a 1 pound weight, the 1 pound weight will feel light.

By priming your system to lift a heavy weight, doing an exercise with a lighter weight feels easy. This phenomenon is called post activation potentiation. You can take advantage of this by doing a heavy bench press or a challenging pushup like a one-armed pushup a few minutes before your workout.

When you go to do your pushups, because your nervous system has been primed to engage extra muscle fibers against a heavy resistance, suddenly just doing ordinary pushups will feel much easier than normal and you'll be able to do many more of them.

Remember, the goal is not to exhaust yourself but to prime your body to be as fresh and powerful as possible. So, despite the temptation to do more, just do one heavy repetition. Don't go to muscular failure, or you won't be mentally or physically fresh to break your old pushup record.

If you don't have any weights around and don't want to do one-armed pushups, that's okay because you can still prime your system for a maximum effort.

Flex and contract every muscle in your body as hard as you can for 10 seconds. Make sure to especially focus on flexing your chest and triceps. Try to flex harder and harder continuously, then, at the end of the 10 seconds, relax fully.

Your body and mind have been charged up and

prepared to fully engage. When you dive into your pushups, they will feel much easier than normal.

This is also a great trick for arm wrestling. Always charge up your arm, flexing it before the match starts so that your arm is ready to explode into a peak contraction instantly by engaging every muscle fiber you've got!

#6 Test Taking

Techniques

"If we did all the things we are capable of, we would astound ourselves." - Thomas Edison

You can do more pushups by improving the efficiency of your form, increasing your stability and minimizing wasted energy. While these techniques can take time to master, you will see the difference the very first time you try them. Even if your physical fitness test or pushup contest starts in a few minutes, there's still time to dramatically improve your performance by applying these techniques!

Bare Foot

It's much harder to do pushups with your hands on
an unstable platform like a yoga ball or a mattress,
because your muscles have to work against the
unsteady surface to stabilize you. Likewise, it's
harder to do pushups with your feet on an uneven
surface for the same reason!

Despite this, most people unknowingly sabotage
themselves by choosing to put their feet on unstable
platforms during their pushup test!

Most athletic shoes have thick cushioning
throughout the shoe to pad and protect your foot
against impact. This is great to prevent long-term

injuries from constant pounding, but it's the exact opposite of what you want when you're doing pushups. This padding is like doing pushups with your feet on a mattress, and it forces your body to work overtime in order to stabilize you against the unstable cushioning of your shoes.

You don't want your shoes to absorb force. You want to make sure that every ounce of force that your body is putting out is going directly into the floor and nothing is being absorbed by the cushioning in your footwear.

Unless the test specifically bans it, always do your pushups barefoot. This keeps your body as stable as possible, so your muscles don't have to waste energy stabilizing you. It also makes sure all the force you put out goes directly into the floor. To get the most out of it, grip the floor with your toes to fully lock your body in place with the most stability possible.

Even if your pushup test requires that you wear shoes, you can still increase your stability. The less padding your shoe has the less force will be wasted and absorbed by your footwear. Weight lifting shoes work well, but they can be expensive and hard to find. Any thin soled, unpadded shoe will work well. For strength training, I'm a fan of Chuck Taylor Converse All Stars™. They are inexpensive, easy to find shoes with thin, dense soles, and they ensure that almost all your force will go straight into the floor.

Keep in mind that the better your shoes are for strength training, the less comfortable they will be for running. So, if you're doing a full physical test including pushups and running, make sure that you bring a change of shoes so that you're ready for the different events.

All these same principles also work for weight lifting. If you normally hit the squat rack in sneakers, next time throw on a pair of Chucks. Watch your squat, leg press, and deadlift increase instantly without the cushioning of your sneakers destabilizing you and soaking up the force your muscles are putting out!

No Restrictions

Pushing your muscles until failure is strenuous, and I'll often see people straining their necks up in the air as they try to force the rest of their body up. It's also common for people to slouch and let their head hang down. Don't crane your neck up or down. It's okay to get a quick sideways glance in the mirror to check your form, but continuously looking sideways can strain your neck and back muscles as well as restricting your air flow.

This is especially true if you strain your head up with the effort of your exertion. If you lean your head back, you can feel your skin pulling tightly against your windpipe. This causes you to unintentionally take shallow breaths and get winded and tired faster

during your workout. For best results, keep your

head in line with the rest of your body so that you

can breath deeply, stay energized, and avoid straining

your neck or back.

Breathe Easy

During your pushup, as you lower your chest down

to the ground, breath in gradually. Let your belly and

chest expand and fill with air. As you pushup off the

ground, exhale the air and let your stomach and

chest deflate.

This breathing pattern accomplishes 3 important

goals: 1) It helps keep your breathing regular so that your muscles get a steady energy supply; 2) It lets you breathe more deeply so that you pull in more oxygen with each breath 3) As you inhale fully, you'll notice that your chest will expand out by a few inches as your rib cage fills with air.

By expanding your chest, you will have a shorter distance to travel to touch the ground. Saving a few inches may not sound like much, but that distance and muscular demand is multiplied by every single pushup that you do.

If you can do 50 pushups normally and can make 10% of them easier, then you just added another 5 pushups to your maximum instantly, just by making your form more efficient. So, time your breathing so that your chest is fully expanded with air at the bottom of the movement to strategically minimize your range of motion and maximize the number of pushups that you can complete.

Valsalva Maneuver

If you are doing a single repetition of a difficult pushup, it can help to take a deep inhale, fill your lungs, and hold your breath throughout the repetition. Filling your chest with air stabilizes your body and is known as the Valsalva maneuver.

Breathing out deflates your chest and decreases your

stability during the range of motion. By holding your breath, your body will be more rigid so that your chest and arms won't have to work as hard to stabilize you, and you can just focus on the lift. Even holding your breath, you will still have enough oxygen for a single rep.

If you're going for a low number of reps, you can also breath in at the top of each rep and hold it throughout the movement, then pause to catch your breath again at the top before you start your next repetition. This power-lifting technique is effective, but it does increase your blood pressure, so it's not recommended for anyone prone to high blood pressure or heart disease.

Also, this technique is not recommended when completing high numbers of reps. It's ideal for difficult pushups like one-armed pushups, lifting heavy weights, and to help you to squeeze out those last few final pushups by stabilizing your torso at the end of your set when your chest and arms are almost exhausted.

Chest Out

Different types of bench presses emphasize different muscle groups. Incline bench press emphasizes the shoulders and upper chest, flat bench press emphasizes the middle chest and the decline bench press emphasizes the lower chest and triceps.

Virtually everyone can decline bench press much more than they can flat or incline bench press because the lower chest muscles are naturally stronger than the upper chest and shoulders.

Hunching your shoulders and leaning forward places more weight on your weaker upper chest and shoulders and limits the number of pushups you can complete. Instead, stick your chest as far forward as you can to replicate a decline press.

This is key for two reasons: 1) Sticking your chest out lets you use your strongest muscle groups for the pushup and 2) Sticking your chest out as far as you can also reduces the total distance your chest has to travel to touch the ground between repetitions.

Increasing the efficiency of your range of motion means that you don't waste strength or energy, allowing you to do more pushups even with the same amount of strength you have today.

Explode

Everyone doing pushups will fail at one of two points, either at the bottom of the movement, which emphasizes the chest, or in trying to straighten and lock out their arms, which strains the arms/triceps. If you tend to fail on lockout, there is a trick that bench press power lifters use that will let you squeeze out a few more reps past the point when you would normally fail.

Momentum is your best friend. It's hard to push a car from a dead stop, but, once you get it moving, it's easy to keep it going. For instance, you may not be able to slowly force your arms to lockout on another pushup. But, if you focus on pushing explosively with as much force as fast as you can at the bottom of the pushup movement, your triceps will only need to put out a small amount of force to keep the motion going and to get you to a full lockout.

This explosive force will wear out your chest, but, if your triceps are your weak point, you need your chest to step up and pick up the slack so that you can get those last few reps when it counts.

Muscular Activation

Normally, when we do an exercise, we don't enlist every available muscle to help us. For instance, you don't just use the front of your chest muscles for pushups, your chest muscles extend out to the bottom and sides of your chest from underneath your armpits. If you want to use your muscles fully, you need to focus on activating them and using them to push.

To see what contracting those muscles feels like, take your hand and put it on your chest with your fingers under your armpit.

Now, fully extend your free hand forward and down.

Do you feel your chest and armpit muscles contracting? Practice that motion until you are in touch with those muscles and can flex them. Feel yourself pushing out from your armpits when you do pushups, and you will fully engage every muscle in your chest to push. This is a power-lifting trick that will also translate to a bigger bench press and help get the most out of every chest workout.

Grab the Floor

If you've ever stood on a skate board, trampoline, or surf board, you know how difficult it is to balance on an unsteady platform. The less stable the platform is, the harder your muscles have to work to stay upright. You are only as strong as the surface on which you are doing pushups. Try and see how many pushups you can do with your hands on a yoga ball or thick couch cushion, and you'll see what I mean!

By tensing your fingers and gripping the floor, you will give your upper body a more stable foundation so that each repetition is less demanding, enabling you to do more of them. Any work that your fingers do to stabilize you is work that your chest and arms won't have to do, which they can save for more pushups. So, to get the most pushups you can, grip the floor!

Irradiation

Try an experiment, place one hand on the forearm of the opposite hand. Grip your forearm tightly below the elbow. Now, flex the bicep of the arm you are grabbing. You'll notice that when you flex your bicep, your forearm muscles also contract. This phenomenon is called **irradiation**—muscular contractions in one body part cause a ripple effect to flow to other nearby parts. Remember, everything in our bodies is connected.

This is important for two reasons:

1) If you are struggling to complete a particularly difficult exercise like a one armed pushup or to get a few final reps out at the end of your set, you can flex

all the muscles in your upper body. When you flex your hands, forearms, and shoulders, they will force extra blood into your chest and triceps, helping them contract harder to squeeze out a few more repetitions.

2) By flexing the rest of your body, you stabilize your body with your core. The more stable your body is, the less work your chest and arms waste holding your body in place. That's extra energy that they can save and use for more pushups. So, keep your core, butt, legs, and back contracted and tight. As you flex one muscle group, it will help everything around it contract; the more rigid and stable your body is the less work your chest and arms will have to do stabilizing you for each pushups.

Efficient Range

of Motion

Pushups are the same as running hurdles in the Olympics. If you have a line of 20 inch hurdles, and you jump 20 inches in the air, you clear them. You're good. Jumping 25 inches is an unnecessary waste of waste of time and energy that could be spent going further or faster. Even with the same amount of strength and endurance you have today, you'll be able to do more pushups with better, more efficient pushup technique that doesn't waste any unnecessary effort or time in the motion.

It takes more energy to walk a mile than to walk a block. The further distance you travel, the more energy you use, and the more demanding it is on your body. This is just as true for pushups as it is for anything else.

Using the same technique that champion power lifters use on the bench press, we can **severely** restrict our range of motion on pushups so that we have less distance to cover, while still maintaining the good form that meets the requirements of most pushup tests.

Stick both arms straight out in front of you. Reach one palm out in front of you as far as you can, now work the other arms shoulder blade back to bring

your palm as far back as you can while keeping your

arm straight.

15-25% Less
Range of Motion

You generally have to touch your chest to the ground for each pushup, but by tucking your shoulders back, you can bring your chest **much** closer to the ground and limit your range of motion.

This will help everyone do more pushups, and the longer your arms are the more it will help you. Push both of your shoulders back, like you're trying to squeeze a quarter between your shoulder blades.

Bringing your shoulder blades back and together

stabilizes you and lets you limit your range of

motion by as much as 6-12 inches, which can easily

be 15%-25% of the total range of motion of your

pushup!

As mentioned above, when you go for a run, it's harder for your legs to carry you 3 miles than 2 miles. Likewise, it's harder for your muscles to push you up 30 inches than 20 inches. By intentionally restricting your range of motion you can dramatically increase the number of pushups you can do.

This technique is also essential for bench pressing, and I've seen lifters add 25% to their maximum bench press weight the the first time they try this technique! Most other people will be traveling an unnecessary extra distance and wasting time and energy on every pushup. Your pushups will be completely efficient, traveling only the minimum required distance while your shoulders help stabilize your chest and arms.

Mix It Up

As long as you maintain the test or contests requirements, you will have some flexibility to adjust your form during the test. Standard pushups work several muscles, but the majority of the strain is placed on your chest and triceps. When you start to get exhausted, pay attention to exactly which muscles are giving out.

If your triceps get tired and can't lock out your straight arms to complete the pushup, switch over to doing some wide pushups, which emphasize your chest and pectorals and give your triceps a break.

When your chest starts to give out and you're struggling to push your chest off the ground at the bottom of the pushup movement, switch over to doing diamond pushups with your hands together in the center of your chest to emphasize your triceps, giving your chest a break.

You can keep bouncing back and forth like this, letting one set of muscles rest while you use the other. You will eventually exhaust both muscle groups completely, but this method will can buy you a good amount of time and extra repetitions, particularly when you're at a point when you cannot do anymore standard pushups without stopping.

US military pushup tests require that you keep both your hands on the ground throughout the test. So you should not pick your hands completely off the ground to reposition yourself. Instead, slide your hands in to the wide or narrow pushup stance you want.

Rest Between Reps

Your body is smart. When you move your body in one direction, the muscles that go in the opposite direction automatically relax so that they don't fight your motion. When you push your hands in front of you in a pushup movement, you engage your chest and triceps and force your back and biceps to relax.

Do More Pushups

When you pull your arms back toward you in a rowing motion, you engage your back and biceps and force your chest and triceps to relax. The more a muscle relaxes and stretches out, the more energy it conserves and the harder it can contract the next time you use it.

Most people miss out by letting gravity do the work of pulling them down between pushups. Don't miss the opportunity to relax your chest and triceps between every pushup. Instead of just letting gravity force you down, engage your back and biceps and actively pull yourself down toward the ground. This gives your chest and triceps a momentary break, helping them to relax so that they can fully contract on the next repetition.

This technique works just as well on every other exercise. After you do a pullup, instead of letting gravity pull you down from the bar, you can push yourself down and give your back and biceps a break. You can pull the bar toward your chest when you do the bench press and relax your chest and triceps.

When you work your opposing muscle groups, you don't want to explosively bounce them, just engage them enough to give your primary muscle group some quick rest between each repetition.

Pace Yourself

Do More Pushups

Many pushup tests are a measure of the maximum number you can do in a limited period of time like 1 or 2 minutes. That may not sound like a long time, but less than 1% of the population can do 2 full minutes of pushups without stopping. Sprinting takes more out of you than walking does. If you try to explosively bang out pushups as quickly as possible you will inefficiently waste a great deal of energy and burn yourself out early in the test.

You can do more pushups, more efficiently if you do pushups at a consistently pace throughout the test. You can still pause to rest, but you shouldn't push so hard that you have to completely stop due to exhaustion half way through your test.

Before you start your pushup test or contest, you need to have an idea of how many pushups you can do within the time limit. You want to pace yourself accordingly because it takes much longer for your muscles to recover from an all out effort, than from mild exertion.

Going up a flight of steps might not even make you breath heavily, but sprinting a few blocks after your missed bus can leave you panting for air for a minute or longer. So don't push yourself to exhaustion until the end of your test. Aim for quick sets that you can quickly recover from.

For example, if you do sets of 15 easily and a set of 30 if you really push, often you're better sticking to sets of 15 between rests. This way, you can minimize your rest breaks, and you won't fully exhaust yourself until the very end of the test.

If you go for an all out effort at the beginning, you'll burn yourself out and either have your arms give out from under you or be so exhausted that you can only squeeze sets of a few reps in for the rest of your test. Also, as your muscles get tired, forcing out each pushup can become agonizingly slow. It's better to rest while you catch your breath, refocus and let your muscles re-energize.

Don't go for broke until the very end of your test, unless you can realistically do pushups the entire time without stopping. Before your pushup test, practice and find a pace that you can maintain

consistently throughout the test with just a few

evenly spaced breaks.

Rest Right

In most pushup tests, they'll let you adjust your

position to rest briefly between repetitions. Always

find out beforehand what the exact rest policies are.

That way, you can get the most out of them, and you

will not inadvertently disqualify yourself on a

technicality. Moreover, if you can sit on the ground

and take all the weight off your upper body, you'll

recover faster than if you are required to maintain a

pushup position throughout the test.

In US military pushup tests, nothing other than your feet and hands can touch the ground at any point during the test. Even if this is the case, when you can no longer complete another pushup, you can still give yourself some quality recovery time.

Lean forward and shift your body weight onto your shoulders to give your primary pushup muscles— your chest and triceps—a quick break. As you wear out you can get the most out of your rest by leaning forward and resting on your shoulders at the top of your pushup, between reps.

Side Foot

If you stand a deck of cards up on its side, just nudging it with your finger is enough to push it over. It doesn't have much surface area, so its base is unstable. On the other hand, if you set the same deck of cards flat on a table and nudge it with your finger, it's almost impossible to tip over onto its side. The wider the base is, the more stable it is.

You can take advantage of this concept with your foot placement when you do pushups. The more stable your feet are, the less strength and energy you will waste steadying yourself on every pushup.

Unless the pushup test or contest specifically requires it, don't do pushups off your toes. Set the **sides** of your feet flat on the ground so your left and right feet are pointed out in opposite

directions. Instead of just having your toes on the

ground, the whole side of your foot has contact with

the ground.

Standard Foot Placement

Side Foot Placement

This stance gives you a much wider, more stable platform and brings your body closer to the ground so that you don't have to go as far to touch your chest to the ground. Depending on your flexibility, this technique can strain your ankles, so don't use this stance if it causes you discomfort.

If your feet slide at all, you may want to wear shoes that are designed so that the sides of the soles aren't smooth and have plenty of grip. You can also grip the floor with the side of your toes and feet for more stability. The more stable and wider your base, the less effort each pushup will take and the more you will be able to do!

Wide Legs

When you do a normal pushup with your feet together, you have gravity pushing against your full height from head to toe. By shortening that length, you reduce the leverage working against you and you don't have to apply as much force or exhaust your muscles as much with each pushup.

The longer a surface is, the more the leverage pushes down against it. That's why standard pushups are so much harder than doing pushups off your knees. Pushups off your knees shorten the length of your body that you have to push, minimizing the leverage working against you. What if you could get this same leverage benefit while doing standard, fully extended pushups?

As long as your pushup test or contest doesn't have specific restrictions on foot placement, you should always spread your feet as wide as possible for your pushups. This is helpful for 2 reasons:

1) This will give you a wider and more stable base so that you don't have to waste upper body strength and energy stabilizing yourself.

2) By spreading your feet wide, you decrease the distance from your hands to your feet, thereby reducing the leverage working against your chest. Even if you're not particularly flexible, this will deeply reduce the distance

from your hands to your feet and greatly

reduce the force and energy required to do

every pushup so that you can do many more.

#7 Conclusion

"There is nothing noble about being superior to some other man. The true nobility is in being superior to your previous self." - Hindu Proverb

Strength isn't just how many pushups you can do. Strength is how you approach all the opportunities for improvement in your life. Keep working hard, keep getting knocked down, keep getting back up. Wake up stronger than you went to sleep, every day!

I hope the techniques I've covered help you as much as they've helped me. Whether your goals are general fitness, challenging friends to contests, or acing your physical test requirements, you have everything that you need to achieve your objectives.

If you've found the methods I've shared to be valuable, please teach them to others. Good luck, I wish you every success in training and in life.

- Barry Rabkin

Made in the USA
Middletown, DE
10 January 2023